ORDINARY
SERVANT

LESSONS IN LOVING JESUS
AND SERVING HIS PEOPLE

ED TAYLOR

ORDINARY
SERVANT

LESSONS IN LOVING JESUS
AND SERVING HIS PEOPLE

ED TAYLOR

ABOUNDING GRACE
MEDIA

ABOUNDING GRACE MEDIA

18900 E. HAMPDEN AVE • AURORA, CO 80013 • (303) 628-7200

Ordinary Servant:
Lessons in Loving Jesus and Serving His people
By Ed Taylor

Copyright ©2016 by Ed Taylor

Published by
ABOUNDING GRACE MEDIA

ISBN: 978-0-9965723-3-0

Printed in the United States of America.

All Scripture quotations, unless otherwise noted, are taken from the New King James Version®. Copyright ©1982 by Thomas Nelson, Inc. Used by permission. All rights reserved.

ABOUNDING GRACE MEDIA
18900 E. HAMPDEN AVE.
AURORA, CO 80013
(303) 628-7200

CONTENTS

CHAPTER 1

GOD USES ORDINARY PEOPLE

GOD WANTS TO USE YOU!

God wants to use you! He wants to use you to make a difference in the world. Have you wondered what it might look like to be that man or woman who makes an impact in the world? Would you say that your heart burns to be used by God? I have good news for you: God wants to use you, and He wants to use you under the banner of "servanthood"!

When we feel that desire and calling to serve in our hearts, we need to pay attention to it and act upon it. It is something to nurture. That commitment to do anything and go anywhere for God is in all of us.

As we spend time studying servanthood, it's my hope that this book will train, equip, and prepare you to be all that

God wants you to be—as we look at the Scriptures and shed the light of His Gospel on your life. I also hope the message in this book will help build like-mindedness with your church body as you serve there.

As we begin this chapter, we'll see the first facet of servanthood: that God uses ordinary people. Perhaps you thought serving Jesus was only for certain people or that there were certain things you needed to know. The reality is simple: you were created to serve.

Picture a diamond. Just as a diamond has many facets that reflect varying levels of light, so servanthood—that calling, that desire, that commitment—also has different sides and varying dimensions. God uses a variety of facets with ordinary people (which we are), and through these facets we see what God is looking for. Ultimately, the shape of the diamond reflects the brilliance of the light. Over the next few chapters, we will learn some of what the Bible teaches about servanthood. It's all about reflecting from the heart the one true light...Jesus! I pray that learning to serve - and serve well - is one of the best times in your spiritual life.

CREATED TO SERVE

In Ephesians 2:8-10, as believers in Jesus we are taught some foundational truths about salvation:

> *"For by grace you have been saved through faith, and that not of yourselves; it is the gift of God, not of works, lest anyone should boast. For we are His workmanship, created in Christ Jesus for good works, which God prepared beforehand that we should walk in them."*

In those simple verses, we see our grace-relationship with God and we learn two things: that we love Him because He first loved us, and that we have been created to serve.

Going forward let's remember that the Bible constantly makes it clear that we haven't been saved *by* good works, but we have been saved *for* good works, so that if we aren't currently serving, we aren't really living up to the potential that God designed and made us for. We were created to serve to make an eternal and lasting difference in this world.

Servant of All

God has chosen you to be His servant. With that job there is a specific pathway laid out. We see some of it in Mark 9:33-35:

> *Then He came to Capernaum. And when He was in the house He asked them, "What was it you disputed among yourselves on the road?" But they kept silent, for on the road they had disputed among themselves who would be the greatest. And He sat down, called the twelve, and said to them, "If anyone desires to be first, he shall be last of all and servant of all."*

If you want to be great in God's kingdom, then your job is to be a servant of everyone. This means that it's our privilege to serve Jesus in the context of our local church *and* in every other place our lives take us. Wherever we are, we are serving the Lord. As a mom changing a diaper, you are serving the Lord. In the workforce, in your school, on patrol, driving a truck, you are serving the Lord. In the book of Mark, we get some insight into how this looks:

> *But Jesus called them to Himself and said to them, "You know that those who are considered rulers over*

*the Gentiles lord it over them, and their great ones
exercise authority over them. Yet it shall not be so
among you; but whoever desires to be great among
you shall be your servant. And whoever desires to be
first shall be slave of all. For the Son of Man did not
come to be served, but to serve and to give His life a
ransom for many."* (Mark 10:42-45)

The word "servant" in this section of Mark is the Greek
word *diakonia.* It's where we get a very familiar word:
deacon. As we dig deeper, we find that *diakonia* is really
a transliteration of a Greek word meaning, "to wait on."

This brings to mind the idea of a waiter or waitress in a
restaurant. Have you ever had a waiter or waitress who was
really good at their job? We've all had the ones who disappear
into the kitchen, only to show up when we're ready to pay.
What about the ones who never let your drink get low, and
who are ready with everything you need? They're good
because they are focused and attentive. *That* is what Jesus is
telling us He expects us to be like: very observant, focused,
and attentive to the needs of others.

There are a few other words in the Bible that surround the
idea of servanthood. One ancient phrase is "in the dust,
laboring." We also see the ideas of being an under-rower, a
co-laborer, and an attendant. All of these words help to fill
out the concept and remind us that being a servant is hard,
laborious work, and that we are entrusted to take care of the
business of the things of God. As servants in His kingdom,
we do not do things the same as the world, we just serve.

Jesus saw the system of leadership in the secular world. He knew that it was about stepping on others and showing off your abilities to get ahead. That's why He made it clear that His kingdom has a different system. His followers serve in a new way. They look and sound differently. They are observant, service-oriented and hardworking. They are great servants!

Once we realize that we are part of a different kind of system, we call ourselves servants. Paul took this concept and deepened it in an important way. He added the idea of commitment. Many times you'll read Paul's letters and see him describe himself as a *bondservant*. This word isn't relevant to our culture, but in Paul's time, it was well known and understood. There were many slaves and masters in the Roman Empire, and this relationship was often a work-related one that had a beginning and an end. A person would make a contract to work for a certain amount of time to work off debt or for other reasons. When the contract was complete, the servant was allowed to leave. Sometimes the relationship between the master and servant was so good that the servant would voluntarily decide to stay with the master, continuing the relationship even though he had the freedom to leave. The Greek word for this is *doulos, a* "bondservant."

Do you want to be a servant of Jesus? I hope you're ready to go deep, making a voluntary, willing commitment to become a bondservant. This is important for us because God has gifted us and saved us. He's bought you with a price. But it's ultimately up to you to make the commitment to be a *bondservant to Jesus Christ*. We see this from Paul's example—it's not only an identity, but it is a way of life.

IT'S FOR EVERYONE

In Mark chapter 10, Jesus says:

> *"And whoever of you desires to be first shall be slave of all. For even the Son of Man did not come to be served, but to serve and to give His life a ransom for many."* (Mark 10:44-45)

If you happen to have an old King James Bible, you'll notice that the word "servant" in Mark 10:43 is translated *minister.* The words *servant* and *minister* are often used interchangeably in the Bible. Unfortunately, when we hear the word "minister" we might dismiss ourselves from the conversation because we think: "Well, I'm never going to be a pastor or a minister, so this isn't for me."

Before we write ourselves off, let's take a moment to reconsider the translation of "servant" as *minister.* This word is not describing an office or a responsibility. It's more focused on describing a lifestyle of service to others based on our love of God. It refers to all of us who are following Jesus. Jesus said He didn't come to be served, but to serve and give his life as a ransom for many (Matt.20:28). With *that*, all believers are ministers of the Gospel and servants of all people.

Weak, Foolish Things

Now that we know every believer is called to be a servant of Jesus and to live a lifestyle of service, I have some good news for you: God has chosen you because you are ordinary!

> *For you see your calling, brethren, that not many wise, not many mighty, not many noble, for God has chosen the foolish things of the world, the weak things of the world, to put to shame the things which are*

mighty, the base things, and the things which are not to bring to nothing the things that are, that no flesh should glory in His presence. (1 Corinthians 1:26-29)

This passage is key in understanding why God wants us, ordinary people, to accomplish His extraordinary purposes. This is where we find good news for everyone who *didn't* score high on their SAT or graduate from school. This is for those who were picked *last* for the team, and for all those who have been overlooked or under-served in life. There is hope for us all. Let's look at it piece-by-piece.

Not Many Wise

This is the first section of 1 Corinthians 1:26, and as we read it we see that among God's people we won't find many people who are wise, scholarly, and smart. It's important to notice that it says *not many,* but it doesn't say *not any.* God's people do include smart people who have significant degrees. That's fantastic! But *not many.*

Not Many Mighty

After wisdom, we see strength. By "*not many* mighty," we're referring to people with significant authority and responsibility in the world today. These are people with positions of power in business and government. Jesus looks at His church, and He says that *not many* people who have a lot of worldly power are here. He doesn't say *not any,* so there are business owners, CEOs, doctors, and government officials. But *not many.*

Not Many Noble

This next aspect refers to our family history. We all have our immediate family history, our upbringing, and our family tree. While a few of us in God's family can look at our upbringing and family tree with pride, *not many* of us do. Some are noble, but *not many.*

We can see that the church of Jesus is made up of ordinary people. There are some very successful people, there are some very smart and very significant people, but *not many.* Why? The answer is in the final section of this verse:

> God has chosen the foolish things of the world to put to shame the wise. (1 Corinthians 1:27)

This is a life verse for so many of us, isn't it? Because this is where we find ourselves described. It's good news! Do you ever feel weak? God has chosen you. Do you ever feel foolish? God has chosen you. Do you ever feel insignificant? God has chosen you to put to shame the wise "that no flesh should glory in His presence" (1 Corinthians 1:29).

I can tell you that this verse is a banner of my life. When people who grew up with me learn that I'm pastoring and involved in a ministry like Calvary Aurora, they are literally shocked. They are shocked that I'm still alive and not in jail somewhere, and they are shocked that I'm a pastor. God chose a fool to bring significant shock to the people who I grew up with. It's the same thing for you. There are people who look at your status in life right now and are shocked. They wonder what happened to you. Then you tell them about God...and He gets all the glory for the great things He has done.

If you begin to take the glory for what God has done, you will be taking the first step of falling away from the Lord. If you glory in your ability to study, to build and fix things, to lead or sing, then you should remember that *no flesh can glory in His presence.* You can only do those things because God gave you that brain, those hands, and those abilities.

When you recognize that God has chosen *you* and He is using *you*—the foolish, weak, insignificant, despised—you realize truly that *no flesh can glory in His presence.* God gets all the attention, all the glory, and all the credit. That's what our service is all about.

Ordinary People

It's been said, and I believe it to be true, that God isn't looking so much for your *ability* as He is looking for your *availability.* God looks at your heart (1 Samuel 16:7), and that's where the work begins. He is looking for a willing and ready heart. Sometimes God's people are held back from service because they feel like they need to be perfect in order to serve Him or be used by Him. If that were true, the Gospel would have never left the Garden of Eden. It would have never left Palestine. It would have never gotten to you and me...because there are no perfect vessels. We can clearly see this when we read about the lives of Adam and Eve, Sarah, David, Rahab, and other people in the Bible.

We all can put up a front to hide what's going on inside—we can smile, put on our best clothes and pretend to be humble—but God knows our hearts. That is always where the work of God starts. It's important to understand that *the condition of your life can make you unavailable to God.* Unconfessed, unrepentant sin can keep us from serving God. If you're mistreating your wife or your husband or your kids, or if you're mistreating yourself in sinful ways, then you are *not* someone God can use. If you are puffed up with pride or resistant to God, then that is where you will stay.

God has so much He wants to do through you. The people around you don't know your heart, but God does. He is ready to start working there today. He'll shape you and mold you and conform you into the image of Jesus Christ. This means He will begin to actively break you. You will have a choice at every moment to give in and surrender, to become completely broken, because that's His heart. He doesn't want you filled with sin, mistreating yourself and others, puffed up with pride. He wants you broken. Why? Because God can bring you up in brokenness. When you're broken, you cry out to God. When you're broken you're dependent. When you're broken, you're open and available. God can heal you when you're broken and make you into something incredible.

Do you remember the story of Jeremiah going to the potter's house? The potter was a person who worked with clay and made plates and cups and pots to hold water. Jeremiah went into the potter and watched him. As he watched the potter work, he noticed that the thing the potter was working on became marred. So the potter flattened it and made something else. Out of the brokenness, the potter was able to build something beautiful, glorious and useful (Jeremiah 18).

I've heard it said that God *doesn't always call the qualified,* but He does *qualify those He calls.* Healing us from the brokenness of our lives is one way He qualifies us to serve. Are you ready for that today?

God the Initiator

Servanthood is ordained by God. Every day He is actively looking for men and women He can use in His service. He is ready to equip you and train you through on-the-job training from His Word and service.

When it comes to service, God will let you know what you need to do. He is always the initiator—which means that He is drawing people into service, and sending them out to serve. God is ready to use you and when He enlists you in ministry, the work you do at church, at home, in your neighborhood, at your job all makes an eternal difference. You are doing things that are far greater than the span of your life can contain, because God the Initiator has called you and is using you today!

If you're not serving right now, you're missing out on all of this. Maybe you're not sure where to help. Perhaps you needed to take a break and never came back. If you're reading this today, it's time to jump back in!

WHAT GOD WANTS

As we finish this chapter, I would like to focus on some characteristics that God is dedicated to putting in the heart of each of his servants.

Fidelity and Loyalty

Second Chronicles 16:9 tells us that the eyes of the Lord run to and fro throughout the whole Earth, to show Himself strong on behalf of those whose heart is loyal to Him. That's great insight! God the Initiator is looking at everyone on planet earth. He's looking for men and women with fidelity and loyalty to Himself! He's looking for men and women who are worthy of trust.

When we are called and committed to serving God, and when we are about to go out to work for Him, we can begin by saying: "God, I am loyal to You. I am committed to You. I owe you everything and I am your willing, voluntary bondservant."

The ideas of *fidelity and loyalty* seem to be missing in our world today. When was the last time you used those words? For many years you could strike a deal by simply shaking a hand. Have you bought or sold a house recently? Did you do it on a handshake? No! You probably had to sign a huge stack of papers, and that's just one small example of how fidelity and loyalty are missing today.

I still believe that fidelity and loyalty are on the earth today, and I believe that the people who represent it are followers of Jesus. It is because we are committed bondservants of Jesus—we are men and women of our word.

Representatives

> So I sought for a man among them who would make
> a wall and stand in the gap before Me on behalf of the
> land, that I should not destroy it… (Ezekiel 22:30)

The above Scripture gives us another insight into what God the Initiator is looking for. He's looking for men and women who are willing to stand in the gap. These are people who see the needs of their home, their church, and their world— those who are ready to put their lives on the line to serve and help. This Scripture also contains the idea that servants of Jesus recognize their role in bringing people to Him and in representing Him properly to the people around them.

Unfortunately, in Ezekiel 22:30, at the end of the verse God says, *"I found no one."* I hope that won't happen today. I hope when God is actively looking among us for someone to stand and represent Him, that He will find a *willing bondservant.*

Heart After God

There is one final characteristic God is looking for, which is found in 1 Samuel 13:14. This Scripture is sad because God tells King Saul that his kingdom is about to end. But through it we are able to see that there is good news...because we see what God is looking for:

> *But now your kingdom shall not continue. The Lord has sought for Himself a man after His own heart, and the Lord has commanded him to be commander over His people, because you have not kept what the Lord commanded you.*

God is looking for a person whose heart follows after Him. This does not mean that God is looking for a perfect person. In this case, the man God found was David. As we read his history, we know that he was not perfect. But as imperfect as David was, at the end of his life he was known as a *man after God's own heart,* because he ultimately obeyed God and desired that God would be glorified more than anything else.

Stirred Up

These characteristics help us to realize that the service we give and the ministry we fulfill is not doing anyone a favor. We're loyal, truthful servants, representing and obeying God. When we serve, it's not about taking credit for it—it's about being used in the hands of God and remembering that

He enlisted us in ministry. Ultimately, it's about *desiring His glory above all.*

These characteristics are ingredients to pray for in our lives. I believe all these things are necessary, in one degree or another, to be effective servants serving on the behalf of God in the church, at work, and in our neighborhoods and families. We need to have that *doulos* mindset and to pray for a heart of fidelity that is loyal to God. We need to be willing to stand in the gap. *We need a heart after God.*

It's a remarkable thing to be a follower of Jesus. God has significant power to take very ordinary people like you and me and do very extraordinary things in and through them. Why? Not only to reach the lost and bring more people into a saving relationship with Him, but also so He will get all the glory for the great things He continues to do today.

For the ways of man are before the eyes of the Lord, and He ponders all his paths. (Proverbs 5:21)

The eyes of the Lord are in every place, keeping watch on the evil and the good. (Proverbs 15:3)

THINK ABOUT IT

God is thinking about you today. He is ready to mold you and heal you and use you to make an eternal difference in the world.

No matter what your life looks like right now, I hope you see that you've been created to serve, and that you can have a heart that desires to serve. Consider this: God wants to use you even more than you want to be used. If you're reading this and battling the whole idea of serving because there is a lot going on in your life, take comfort because God can turn those things around. He can give you the strength and wisdom you need to step out in faith and serve.

As we finish this chapter, I want you to know I'm praying that God will stir you up. If you've never made a commitment to serve, I hope that you'll make one today. If you've been on the sidelines for a while, I hope you'll get back in the game— If your life is full of difficulties, I pray that God will give you the wisdom, strength, and ability to take care of those things so they can be behind you, and you can step ahead to serve.

I hope we can enjoy the fruit that comes from your life today. Not only for the sake of the church, but for the sake of all eternity, for the sake of our cities, and for the sake of the lost. God is ready to use you to make an eternal, lasting difference in this world. I pray that your desire to serve grows, and that you see your role in what God is doing on the earth today.

CHAPTER 2

HAVING A SHEPHERD'S

AND PASTOR'S HEART

In the first chapter of this book, we focused on the fact that God uses ordinary people to complete His work on earth. Now as you prepare to step out and serve alongside your pastor and shepherd Jesus, it's important to take time to understand the heart of Jesus and learn how to serve alongside Him with a heart unified with Him. The people that we have the privilege of serving belong to Him. He desires to draw them to Himself, so it is vital we see His heart, a pastor's heart.

When we think of the heart, we're not referring to the pumping muscle in the middle of your chest cavity. In the Bible, we learn that the heart is the whole you—and it's who you are in your thoughts, speech, and actions. The heart that Jesus is looking for in us is a *connected heart* that goes out in His strength and wisdom to serve.

This kind of heart is a shepherd's heart—a pastor's heart. It's not a prerequisite for you to be a pastor or have a pastor's calling or role in order to have that kind of heart. This heart is a natural overflow of a life connected with King Jesus. How we serve directly relates to what's in our heart. In this chapter, we'll look at that more.

THE PICTURE: THE POTTER AND THE CLAY

Jeremiah chapter 18 shows us a clear picture of the father-heart of God.

At this time, Jeremiah was serving a nation of people who were resisting God. God wanted to speak to Jeremiah and help him understand his role in this community, so he sent him down to the potter's house.

> *The word which came to Jeremiah from the Lord saying: 'Arise and go down to the potter's house and there I will cause you to hear My words.' Then I went down to the potter's house and there he was, making something at the wheel. And the vessel that he made of clay was marred in the hand of the potter; so he made it again into another vessel, as it seemed good to the potter to make. Then the word of the Lord came to me saying: 'O, house of Israel, can I not do with you as this potter?' says the Lord. 'Look, as the clay is in the potter's hand, so are you in My hand, O, house of Israel!* (Jeremiah 18:1-6)

I love this visual of the potter spinning the clay and shaping it into something that He desires. There are three pictures to keep in mind from this passage. The first is the potter. He's a picture of our loving Heavenly Father. Second is the clay in his hands, which represents us. And finally, there's the wheel, which represents life.

Jeremiah is watching the potter, and notices that while the potter works to create something from the lump of clay on the wheel, there is a problem. The word used here is *marred* and one translation of this word is "ruined," so the clay becomes ruined in the potter's hand.

When the clay became marred, it may have seemed like the potter should have thrown it out, but he saw it as useable and chose to reshape it. We live in a very disposable society, and often it seems easier to throw something away and buy something new than take time to fix it. That mindset can be scary for us, because we all have times in our lives where we become marred or feel ruined because of something that has happened.

This is where Jeremiah's description of the potter gives us insight into the character of God. The potter always saw a use in the ruined clay. So, though the clay became ruined, the potter did not throw the clay out but started over with the same clay. This is a lesson to you that believe in Jesus. You aren't disposable! God does not have plans to toss you aside when ruinous things come; HE is with you all the way.

"Lo, I am with you to the very end, to the ends of the age." (Matthew 28:20)

The wheels of life will spin, and things may come that are ruinous, but you are in the hands of a loving, faithful God. He would rather fix something when it breaks. In Psalm 37, God speaks of how He cares for us:

Delight yourself in the LORD, *and He'll give you the desires of your heart. (Psalm 37:4)*

God is in the business of fixing broken things and when you are ruined, He will make you into something new. This is why there is a great freedom in serving Him when you remember His love, grace, mercy and truth. He will give you His desires.

When you are ready to serve God in your church and in your community, you need to remember that Heaven is going to be filled with every tongue, tribe, nation and background of people. Keep in mind, that they may have been in darkness so long that they don't know how to deal with light, and if you don't understand the fruits of the spirit and have them in your heart, you could end up hurting people in the name of Jesus. This is where you need to understand the Father's heart (one of mercy, compassion, restoration, reconciliation, grace, patience, love, joy, peace, kindness, goodness, faithfulness, and self control), because the people that you will serve need to know His heart too, and the main way they will understand it is Him through you. People matter to God.

THINGS TO THINK ABOUT

Here are some things to think about in your personal life when you look at your heart.

Am I faithful? We know that God is faithful, and faithfulness is a hallmark of everyone who follows Him.

Am I available? God is always available and attentive to your needs, and as you prepare to serve you will extend that same availability and attentiveness to others.

Am I teachable? God will always be instructing you, and when your hands are busy in serving others, being open and ready to receive is vital.

Am I spiritual? A growing relationship with God is essential to service because it puts us in tune with God's pastor's heart and allows us to hear clearly from the Holy Spirit.

Am I ready to be a sacrifice? Jesus laid down His life for you, and when you serve Him, you will be laying down your life for others.

Our hearts are not naturally ready to serve, but evaluating ourselves will begin to prepare us. Once you have done that, there is one more thing you can do to prepare your heart: Pray. Ask God for compassion. Ask God to help you care. Ask God to help you have concern for others. Ask God to help you to see and observe needs, so that you would be selfless. Ask for a soft heart to serve well and thick skin so that you can take things spiritually and not personally. God is ready to answer you and give you a pastor's heart. Now is your time to be ready to step up...by faith.

The Problem: Serving without a Pastor's Heart

In Jeremiah, we are given a beautiful picture of serving with a shepherd's heart. The Bible always gives us both sides of an issue, and in Ezekiel 34, we are given a picture of the negative side of serving. We are given a glimpse of what it looks like to serve without a pastor's heart:

> *And the word of the Lord came to me saying, "Son of man, prophesy against the shepherds of Israel, prophesy and say to them, 'Thus says the Lord God*

to the shepherds, woe to the shepherds of Israel who feed themselves. Should not the shepherds feed the flocks? You eat the fat and clothe yourselves with the wool, you slaughter the fatlings but you do not feed the flock. The weak you have not strengthened, nor have you healed those who were sick, nor bound up the broken, nor brought back what was driven away, nor sought what was lost, but with force and cruelty you have ruled them so they were scattered because there was no shepherd and they became food for all the beasts of the field when they were scattered. My sheep wandered through all the mountains and on every high hill, yes My flock was scattered over the whole face of the earth and no one was seeking or searching for them..." (Ezekiel 34:1-6).

It's clear that these leaders failed, and we can learn a lot from their mistakes.

MISTAKES WE CAN MAKE

1. Selfishness
These leaders took care of themselves instead of the people they were supposed to serve.

2. Used People
These leaders used people for their own gain. These verses say that they took advantage of people bringing their offerings. They took the things that belonged to God and used them to feed and clothe themselves, rather than to care for the people.

3. Took the Best
When they saw something good, they took it instead of feeding it to the flock of people they were caring for.

4. Ignored Needs
We read that: *"The weak they didn't strengthen."* This means that when they saw a need, they turned away from it.

5. Disregarded Pains
This Scripture says: *"nor have you healed those that were sick."* This means that they actively ignored the needs and pains of their flock.

6. Closed their Eyes
The flock was weak, sick and broken. They were desperately in need of a healthy relationship with God, but the leaders closed their eyes, or turned their backs on those who were hurting.

7. They Paid No Attention
Because the flock was sick and weak and broken, they ran away from God. We know that Jesus told us to leave the ninety-nine and go after the one, but they didn't. In fact, they actively ignored the one.

8. They Refused to Help
In the book of Ezra, we see all of the sin going on in Jerusalem. These leaders saw that sin and refused to help or be used by God.

9. They Were Harsh and Angry
The outcome of their sin is that they led by force and cruelty. This means that they represented God as harsh and angry, and God used Ezekiel to tell them that not only

was He not like that, but that He was now against them for misrepresenting him.

10. They were Careless
The final thing we see about these leaders is that they were careless because, *"the people were scattered, they became food for the beast where they were scattered."* They wandered and were lost, and no one searched for them.

These are heavy indictments and they come from God Himself. These leaders lacked the heart of God and no longer saw people as people to serve in their hurting, weak, and broken states. They only saw their own needs and took care of themselves. It is God's expectation that you care for His flock, not as a task, but with a heart that is knit together with His heart.

THE CURE: CARE

When you serve, you can get tunnel vision and miss the main thing—*the people.* When you hold fast to the reminder that Jesus died for every person, you'll understand the heart of Jesus. The bottom line of serving God is that you care—you care about the Lord, and you care about others.

You've read that the greatest commandment is to "love the Lord with your heart, soul and strength." The next part of that commandment is to "love your neighbor as yourself" (Luke 10:27). If you care about your relationship with Jesus, you are going to be filled with grace, truth, justice and righteousness. When the entire fellowship family of believers is filled with those attributes, nothing will hold back the work that God is ready to do. It all begins with caring.

Serving God is not about obtaining titles and position; it's all about serving the Lord, and that means being willing to take the lower position no matter what your title or position might be. When you seek to serve your church community, the only thing you will attain is a deep love-abiding relationship with Jesus. It's an amazing thing to see what you will do as you extend yourself to serve. And it all begins with caring.

THE FOCUS OF OUR SERVICE

If you serve without a caring heart, you'll become like the Pharisees, but when you take hold of the heart of Jesus, you'll become like Him. In Luke chapter 4 Jesus launches His ministry by describing His heart:

> *He came into Nazareth where He had been brought up and as is custom was in when into the synagogue on the Sabbath day and He stood up to read and He was handed the book of the prophet Isaiah and when He had opened the book He found the place where was written, "The Spirit of the Lord is upon me, and He's anointed Me to preach the gospel to the poor, he sent me to heal the brokenhearted, to preach deliverance to the captives and recovery of sight to the blind, to set liberty those who are oppressed and to preach the acceptable year of the Lord."* (Luke 4:16-19)

THINK ABOUT IT

The first thing that you and I need is the fullness of the Spirit of God to serve. When you approach ministry, attending a special seminar on serving or going through a simple Bible study on how to minister to others is not enough. You need the Spirit of God in you and upon you.

Jesus made it clear that His service was to be Spirit-filled. He also showed us that serving is all about people: releasing, saving, preaching and healing people, all under the power of the Holy Spirit. This is how you can have God's heart in serving.

As you pray about serving and getting involved, I'll be praying that you will be a vessel of God with a pastor and shepherd's heart. I hope these simple truths have enlivened and emboldened you to serve Him, with His heart, as you love Him with all your heart, soul and mind. God has a plan and purpose for you and as you step out in faithfulness, He will one day say to you "Well done good and faithful servant, enter into the joy of your Lord" (Matthew 25:23).

CHAPTER 3

SERVING AND SUPPORTING

Pastors and Leaders

G od has ordained godly leadership in His church and in
your life. When you seek to serve in your church with
a heart unified with Jesus, you will encounter a chain of
command that God has created to allow His body to work
in unity.

It's important, as you step out to serve the Lord in any area
of life, that you understand that believers are co-laboring
together under the authority of God. This is especially
important within a church family. No matter what a person's
role or responsibility, no matter what their title, we are all in
this together and we must never forget that.

Clarification of Authority

When people speak about authority and submission, it
makes some of us very uncomfortable. You might wrestle

with the whole thought of submission to authority simply because the authority structures in your life have hurt you. It may have been in the home, in church, in a workplace, or a school. When you've been hurt, hearing someone in leadership speak about submission can bring those things that hurt back up.

UNGODLY AUTHORITY

I want to be very clear about this: when there is ungodly leadership, where there is abuse and pain, where the character and the heart of God are not being represented, *you are under no obligation to submit to such authority.* In that case, you can truly step aside and say, "I serve God and not man."

When there's a sin involved and the leadership isn't acting in a godly way, there is a remedy. The Bible says that if someone has sinned against you, then you're to go to that person alone and share that offense, eye-to-eye and face-to-face—not in an e-mail or a text message. Go to them, share your heart with them (Matthew 18:1).

Do you know what happens then? Ninety-nine percent of the time, God resolves the problem right then and there. If that doesn't work, then there's *another* provision. The Bible says to go back, taking two other godly people with you. They are there to be a godly witness to the situation as you plead your case.

If that doesn't work, then there's provision for the leadership of the church to get involved. Finally, if that doesn't work, the leadership of the church will remove that rebellious, unrepentant person...if church discipline is necessary.

The beautiful thing is that if the person hears you, God has rescued them from their sinful activity. You've won them back and now there will be healing and health and growth.

GODLY AUTHORITY

We've just learned about how to respond to ungodly leadership. However, when there is godly, Jesus-honoring leadership and oversight, we are to match it with godly submission. That's how God has put the structure of His Church together. He's given us leaders, and He's given us the heart and desire to submit to them.

What Does the Bible Say?
The Bible has several important things to say about church leadership.

> *Let the elders who rule well be counted worthy of double honor, especially those who labor in the word and doctrine.* (1 Timothy 5:17)

> *Obey those who rule over you, and be submissive, for they watch out for your souls, as those who must give account. Let them do so with joy and not with grief for that would be unprofitable for you. (Hebrews 13:17)*

> *Likewise you younger people, submit yourselves to your elders. Yes, all of you be submissive to one another, and be clothed with humility, for God resists the proud, but gives grace to the humble. (1 Peter 5:5)*

In just these scriptures you can see that God has ordained the leadership and authority in your life. Every person is under authority, and the Bible makes it clear that God has put people in your life—a pastor, a leader, a parent—so that when you get off track, they will take the time to love you by letting you know. When they do that, your response should be to receive from them as unto the Lord. Pray through what they told you, and take the opportunity to grow as a servant of God.

GODLY SUBMISSION

We're all under authority in different areas of our lives. Sometimes you will disagree with the authorities in your life. We've looked at what to do when the authorities are ungodly in their leadership. That does happen, but more often the issue is a minor disagreement where you don't see eye-to-eye.

Disagreements with authorities in your life happen outside of church as well. You might disagree with your boss or your neighborhood association, and feel that you would handle things differently. Take a minute to check your heart and see if you are unsubmissive with others in your life. If you can see places in your life that indicate anger and frustration with the authorities in your life, then let me encourage you to cut some slack to the people who are making decisions. When you start serving in church, you will be bringing those feelings with you.

Disagreements happen. We all have different ideas and approaches to the different things we encounter. So if what you are feeling is a simple disagreement, and nothing is wrong, the Bible encourages you to hope the best and think the best about that leader according to 1 Corinthians 13. This is so important. As you're serving, you need to trust that God put those people in your life to speak into it, even if you don't fully agree with them. The Bible is clear: when there's godly leadership, there's to be godly submission.

There is truth in the saying that Jesus is our shepherd. We serve God and not man. It is true, but it can be misused. When disagreements arise or something doesn't happen the way everyone wants, there will always be people who say that they serve God and not man. This can be an excuse for a lack of submission to the leadership God has put in your life and in mine. Sadly, this can lead to a person heading out to do their own thing, their own way, apart from true godly submission. When that happens, it causes confusion and chaos. The division that comes from this attitude has destroyed many churches.

Lack of submission to leadership isn't something new in the church; it happened even when the church was young. If you read through 1 Corinthians, you'll read about people complaining and fighting, and choosing sides. If you boil it down, the issue wasn't about who was following Paul or who was following Cephas. This division was about a true lack of submission to godly leadership.

Let me finish by saying that disagreements are to be worked through. It would be a sad thing to cause division in a church because you have a point of view that the leader didn't see, or something to offer that they didn't know about, or couldn't use right now. Those things happen, but they must not divide us. If they do, then the devil wins.

LIKE-MINDEDNESS

Submission to authority can be difficult, especially if you've been hurt, but when there is like-mindedness, submission will come naturally. Let's explore that further. In Ephesians 5 it says:

> See then that you walk [uprightly or carefully or circumspectly], not as fools but as wise, redeeming the time, because the days are evil. Therefore do not be unwise, but understand what the will of the Lord is. And do not be drunk with wine, in which is dissipation; but be filled with the Spirit, speaking to one another in psalms and hymns and spiritual songs, singing and making melody in your heart to the Lord, giving thanks always for all things to God the Father in the name of our Lord Jesus Christ, submitting to one another in the fear of God. (Ephesians 5:15-21)

In this section of Ephesians, the Holy Spirit is speaking through Paul. You'll notice that before He talks to kids, or parents, or husbands and wives, he speaks to *all* believers. He reminds us to submit to one another.

Paul is referring to a mutual submission that takes place in our relationships with each other, and he is clear that it is very beneficial. It's good for society. It's good for the church of Jesus Christ, and with it comes a natural like-mindedness that we need when we serve together.

What Is Like-mindedness?
Like-mindedness is not conformity. This is good news! We know that God uses ordinary people. That means He wants to use you, with your own personality, upbringing, and individuality. There is an amazing variety of people on the

earth, and I think this is why there is a variety of churches. God is doing a variety of things through different, good, God-fearing, Jesus-honoring churches.

In each church, there are various ministries that are ongoing and vital for the health of the larger body of Jesus. It's clear that you don't need to be *a clone* to serve in like-mindedness with your fellow believers. In fact, the only time the Bible speaks of conformity is when it tells us to be conformed into the image of Jesus (Romans 12:2)—*never another person.* God wants you to be who you are, serving in your place in His church.

Like-mindedness is not blind allegiance. You are never to have the attitude that you are a faithful soldier who doesn't ask questions. Serving in the body of Christ means there is room for your input. There's room for where you are in life, where you've come from, what God's doing in your heart, what God has spoken to you, what you've gained through your devotions, and what you've seen through your Bible reading. These things are valuable in making you the servant God needs.

The word, *like-mindedness,* means to have similar tastes or opinions, and to be *generally be going in the same direction.* The Greek word for like-mindedness, *omopsychías,* comes from two words: *equal* and *soul.* Together they give us the idea of unity, harmony, and general agreement together.

The Bible has plenty of examples of like-mindedness. Jesus was like-minded with His apostles—eleven of them. He spent three years with them, instructing, guiding, correcting and preparing them for ministry. Paul was like-minded with

Timothy and Barnabas. It was a blessing and encouragement
for Jesus and Paul to have these like-minded people serving
with them.

Like-mindedness means that you go in generally the same
direction as your authorities because you see things *generally
the same way.* When disagreements come up, you work them
out, and you move forward for the cause of Jesus Christ. What
a blessing for your church and for your pastor to be serving
alongside people who love the flock and are like-minded!

It can be difficult to remain like-minded, and that's why the
Bible contains many passages with encouragement to help us
remain like-minded as we serve.

> *Now may the God of patience and comfort grant
> you to be like-minded with one another, according to
> Christ Jesus, that you may with one mind and one
> mouth glorify the God and Father of our Lord Jesus
> Christ.* (Romans 15:5-6)

> *...fulfill my joy by being like-minded, having the same
> love, being of one accord, of one mind.* (Philippians 2:2)

Like-mindedness is important in ministry. Lack of like-
mindedness brings confusion and chaos. Paul experienced
this and shows us the sorrow that comes from its lack:

> *For I have no one like-minded, who will sincerely care
> for your state, for all seek their own, not the things
> which are of Christ Jesus.* (Philippians 2:20)

We've already said it, but let me say it again: *where there's
godly leadership, there's to be godly submission.*

Like-mindedness is important for all the different people and different flavors of ministry. You need to find a church and a place in that church where you can be like-minded and say, "That's it. That's where I belong. That's where I want to serve. That's what my heart's desire is."

The Blessing of Like-mindedness

Exodus chapter 17 shows us a picture of what like-mindedness can achieve:

> *Now Amalek came and fought with Israel in Rephidim. And Moses said to Joshua, "Choose us some men and go out, fight with Amalek. Tomorrow I will stand on the top of the hill with the rod of God in my hand." (Exodus 17:8-9).*

When you read this, consider what it was like to be in Joshua's shoes for a moment. There's a big battle going on. The Amalekites are coming and they're attacking Israel. Moses sees the situation, makes a decision, and basically says, "Joshua, go get some men and go down and fight with them. I'm not going to go fight with you. I'm going to go up on the mountain." Now, this is where Joshua could have stepped up and said, "Wait a minute! What?! You're going to go up to the mountain to a safe place while you send me down with some men to do your fighting for you?! You want us to put our lives on the line while you go up to the mountain?!"

Perhaps these would have been good questions to ask, but there was no time for questions. There was a fight going on! If you were in Joshua's shoes and had that kind of frustration come up as a response to Moses, it may reflect an unsubmissive heart.

There's more to this story. The very next words in Exodus17:10 are words that you want to mark in your life:

"So Joshua did as Moses said to him."

Joshua did what Moses asked with no questioning, no hesitation, and no arguing. This was an urgent, difficult situation. Joshua had no idea why Moses was going up while he stayed down, but he submitted and went and fought with Amalek while Moses, Aaron, and Hur went up to the top of the hill.

When we come to the next verses we see what happened:

> *And so it was, when Moses held up his hand that Israel prevailed; and when he let down his hand, Amalek prevailed. But Moses' hands became heavy; so they took a stone and put it under him, and he sat on it. And Aaron and Hur supported his hands, one on one side, and the other on the other side; and his hands were steady until the going down of the sun. So Joshua defeated Amalek and his people with the edge of the sword."* (Exodus 17:11-13)

Now we understand more of the story. Moses had a plan. He had received the orders and direction from God. He told Joshua what he needed him to do and then took Aaron and Hur up to the mountain. God used Joshua's sword and Moses's rod and hands, and the help of Aaron and Hur to bring victory to Israel. It was a group effort, but Joshua had no way to know that until after the battle.

When there is a man or a woman who is following God, demonstrating the fruit of the Spirit, opening the Bible to you, and they give you direction—it is important to obey, even when you don't agree with it. In the heat of the battle sometimes things might happen that you don't fully understand or you don't fully agree with, but if you've seen godly leadership demonstrated, then submit and follow through. You can follow up later. Like-mindedness means that you are willing to do what you're asked to do, even if there's no explanation. You just trust the Lord is in it. I believe that if it's godly leadership, there's going to be fruit like we see here; there will be victory.

I want to be clear that I am in no way advocating that you submit to ungodly, abusive, hurtful leadership. I mentioned this earlier, and it's important to understand that kind of leadership does not reflect the heart of God. When you see that happening, it's necessary for God to intervene and fix that right away.

SERVING STINKS

Aaron and Hur had the job of helping Moses. We can see that they were so in-tune with God and the situation that they were able to help Moses even before they are asked. It's a beautiful picture of how the body of Christ can flow when it is like-minded. There's so much wonderful fruit that comes through service when you've caught the vision and you understand what God's doing through the ministry where you are.

God does some crazy, amazing things through people like us! Here's a lesson though: Ministry stinks at times. In that day, they didn't take daily showers, and there was no deodorant. Aaron and Hur were holding up Moses' arms. The situation was hard and, to be tactful, probably stinky.

That's a very literal example, but know this: when we pray for God to open doors, He will, but some of them are very, very hard. Your heart will break over what sin has done to destroy a life and what sin is currently doing to ruin lives. When you are like-minded with God, the stinkiness of a life won't make you keep someone at arm's length; you'll just dive right in. It's hard. It's difficult. It's self-sacrificing. It can require a lot of time and effort on your part, and it can seem unrewarding. The thankfulness isn't there all the time, and not everybody's happy when you have to tell them hard things; sometimes people leave mad at you, and sometimes people stay mad at you. When you commit to serve, remember that God has given you the opportunity to be a part of those difficulties. Ministry is worth it.

To be honest, sometimes serving alongside your pastor is going to stink. He gets frustrated and goes through things just like you do. That goes for the other lay pastors in a church and the rest of the staff. Normal stuff happens. You've got to be ready for that and not get tripped up by it. The work of the church is to grow together through these challenges and allow God to intervene. When He does, it will bring us back to a 1 Corinthians 13 type of love in our lives.

Pride: The Enemy of Submission
The greatest enemy of godly submission in any life is pride. *Pride* is when we stop thinking of ourselves the way God does and begin thinking too highly of ourselves or too lowly of ourselves. When we get prideful, we forget that we are servants. A good test of your pride is having people actually treat you like a servant.

When your anger begins to rise, remember that you only have one calling and that is to please Jesus. That's it. Whatever God has you doing, I want you to know that it has an eternal effect and value. But if you allow the sin of pride to remain, it will take you out, remove you from usefulness, and separate you from people who love you and want to care for you.

THINK ABOUT IT

Everybody has a place, and the glue that holds us all together is like-minded submission. God does great and wonderful things through a group of people who are knit together in love, serving God wholeheartedly. Nothing can hold back a church filled with those kind of people!

My prayer as we finish this chapter is that God will give you a servant's heart. I pray that He will show you how you can support your pastor and the other leaders in your life. I pray that God will surround you with people who are like-minded in serving the Lord.

CHAPTER 4

VITAL ELEMENTS

FOR EFFECTIVE SERVICE

So far you've seen that when it comes to servanthood, God uses ordinary people. God's plan and desire is for those ordinary people to have a heart like Jesus. In the last chapter, you were reminded that you need to be like-minded with the leadership in your church. In this chapter, we're going to change direction and look at eight ingredients that will help guide your servanthood and keep your eyes on Jesus.

As we open up, it's important to keep in mind that any opportunity you have to serve is a privilege. The word *privilege* in the Bible gives us the idea of "a restricted honor." That means it is a special, restricted honor to serve God, and it's not something to take lightly. When serving God's people is no longer seen as a privilege, when you and

I begin to think that we deserve to serve and we've earned the right to a certain title or position, we are in danger of becoming corrupt in our leadership. Always remember that, according to the scriptures, all we *deserve* is eternal separation from God. It's only His great love for us that has saved us. Spiritual leadership and servanthood are like salvation—they are gifts from God that we receive.

The only thing that will make you effective in service is God's work in the position of your heart and the integrity of your life. As ordinary people who serve God, be very careful to stay away from the idea that you will pay your dues in serving God in certain ways and then get promoted to more important things. We get this idea of promotion from the corporate world. When a person is hired in an entry-level position, their goal is not to remain there, but to get promoted to a higher-level position. Things work a little differently for servants of God in His church. Promotion is *not* our goal, and as we see in Psalm 75, it's not even up to us: *"Promotion comes not from the east or from the west but the Lord raises up one and puts down another."*

The Bible makes it clear: as servants of Jesus, you and I will never pay our dues. We will simply do what needs to be done, from cleaning toilets and picking up trash, to leading worship and discipling others. The work is the same whether you've been a believer 50 years or one day.
Everyone who serves must ultimately be filled with character and integrity. I believe God is looking for leaders who serve well and servants who lead well and together we will reach a lost generation and see people's lives changed!

In 1 Peter 5:1-4 we begin to see what it means to serve God well:

> *The elders who are among you I exhort. I, whom a fellow elder and a witness of the sufferings of Christ and also a partaker of the glory that will be revealed, shepherd the flock of God which is among you serving as overseers, not by constraint but willingly, not for dishonest gain but eagerly, nor as being lords over those entrusted to you, but being examples to the flock. And when the chief shepherd appears you will receive the crown of glory that does not fade away.* (1 Peter 5:1-4)

Spiritual Leaders are Under-Shepherds

There is one pastor of the church and His name is Jesus. Everyone else, from the pastor to the Sunday school teacher, is an under-shepherd. That means that you serve the Chief Shepherd. In 1 Peter 5:1, you'll notice that Peter is talking to a group of leaders called elders, as his peers: "The elders who are among you I exhort. I, whom a fellow elder...". It's important to see that Peter doesn't set himself up as being more important because he had been with Jesus. He doesn't give himself an important title, or demand that they obey him and that's a reality that you never want to lose as you serve God. Peter was with Jesus; he served, grew, and made mistakes. He was discipled by Jesus Himself and that's why it's so key when he reminds us that we are serving in a church that belongs to Jesus.

It was *Jesus* who gave His life to forgive each of us of our sins. We are His servants. We are serving people who belong to Jesus, the "flock of God." We are representing Jesus to our community.

LEADERS WHO SERVE: CHURCH GOVERNMENT

Peter calls himself an elder, and that brings to mind the unfortunate debate in churches today over what type of church government is the right kind of church government. A careful student of the scriptures will find there are various types of church government that certainly could fit in the context of the New Testament because there is no definitive scripture that tells us what church government should be like. That's why you will find elder-run churches and pastor-led churches, and congregation-led churches. Some churches combine more than one style.

Peter doesn't try to set himself up as the only authority, and I think he wants us to understand that it's easy to argue about things that don't really matter. Ultimately we need to allow the Holy Spirit to do what He wants in the local congregation. When it comes to biblical church government, the form is not as important as the character and integrity of the people entrusted with spiritual leadership. Remember, God is looking for leaders who serve and servants who lead!

Spiritual Leaders and Servants are Sheep Too

No matter what your role in God's church is, your first position is that of follower of Jesus. Peter makes this clear when he says, *"shepherd the flock of God which is among you."* You are part of the flock of God. No matter what your role may become, you will always be sheep first. This makes every person in the church equal in the place of servanthood and leadership.

In the corporate world, the leadership model is typically depicted as a pyramid with the president at the top and everyone else filling in below according to their responsibilities. When you look at a church, it's easy to view things the same way, with the pastor at the top and everyone else filling in below. Peter makes it clear that the church of Jesus is different. If you used the pyramid model, it would be inverted, with the people who have the most responsibility becoming the greatest servants. Jesus said that "...*whoever desires to be great among you, let him be your servant*" (Matthew 20:26). If you want to be really great in God's kingdom, you'll find yourself growing in humility and servanthood. It's clear that in God's kingdom, the way up is the way down!

As we serve, it can be easy to forget our place and think that *we* are the shepherd or that a certain church or ministry is *ours*. Here's the reality: you will never be so vital that the church can't move on without you. The church is not ours, and we don't serve in our own authority but with God's. So, no matter what your role is, you should be doing your work for the Lord, filled with His Spirit. That's why any believer can pray over another believer, visit people in the hospital, bring meals and more. God is our pastor and we are all sheep serving Him together.

Spiritual Leaders are Servants
The greatest example we have of a servant is Jesus. In John 13:3-5: "Jesus, knowing that the Father had given all things into His hands, and that He had come from God and was going to God, rose from supper, laid aside His garments, took a towel and girded Himself. After that, He poured water into a basin and began to wash the disciples feet, and to wipe them with a towel with which he was girded."

Jesus is our great shepherd who laid down His life for the sheep and came not to be served but to serve. That's the standard, and it shows us that leaders in the church ought to be the greatest servants of all. There is no other alternative.

When you serve, you need to make things easier for those you are serving. It's a reciprocal relationship that we all have in the church, and it allows the church to become effective.

Spiritual Leaders Serve Willingly

The next thing Peter tells us is that when you serve, you need to serve willingly, and not with constraint. That's what I ask you to do. If you want to serve, then serve your heart out for Jesus.

This can be a place where many people falter, because when you serve, especially within a church, you will get tired because it will be hard. It's hard walking alongside someone, begging them not to divorce their husband. It's hard walking alongside someone begging a husband not to be cruel to his wife. It's hard watching kids go sideways. It's hard seeing what drugs and alcohol will do to a family. It's hard serving people that say they're believers but live like they're unbelievers. It's hard walking alongside someone that's mourning and grieving. It's hard watching a believer getting busted for stealing. On top of all that, being a servant comes with spiritual warfare and other difficulties.

All of that can bring us to a point of feeling burned out. Let me say this: if you are serving in any area of the church, and feeling tired or burned out, *take a break!* Some believers actually wear "burned out" like a badge of honor that shows how hard they are working. In 1 Peter 5:2, Peter tells us to serve *"not by constraint, but willingly."*

One danger that comes with getting burned out is feeling like a ministry belongs to you and can't continue without you. That is a constraint. When you serve, you do things that the Lord leads you to do, but *you* don't do everything. Every ministry seems to have a season, and sometimes I let a ministry end because its season is over. As believers, we let things go because we are not married to ministry, we're married to the Lord. If you are burned out, then you can't serve well. So take some time off before you hurt someone!

Perhaps you were burned out years ago and you've taken time off. Consider serving again before you get too used to resting. The kingdom is ready for you and your giftings and talents. Serve willingly and be like Paul who said, *"Woe is me if I do not preach the gospel..."* (1 Corinthians 9:16).

Spiritual Leaders Serve Honestly
When you serve God's people, your job is to feed the flock, to lovingly care for it, and not to fleece it. Peter says at the end of verse two, "Not for dishonest gain, but eagerly." To put it simply, don't start serving to rip off God's people. When the issue of money comes up, it's sad to say that there are far too many examples of men and women in leadership that take advantage of the church. Let me be clear: that is not the heart of God! That's why the church needs to be careful with who is allowed to serve and become a leader and elder in the church. We don't want people serving under the banner of Jesus to take advantage of the vulnerabilities of the flock. We don't serve for what we can get. We get all we need from Jesus, and then we give to others.

Spiritual Leaders Serve Humbly
As we move on, there's a little phrase Peter gives us in verse three, *"Not as being lords over."* That phrase boils down to

this: in ministry, we don't need any bosses. Ministry is not something to do so that you can have control and power over someone's life. I've met people like that and they don't last. What God's church wants and needs is servants.

Spiritual Leaders Serve As Stewards
In this section of 1 Peter we see so many important things, and here's another from verse three: *"entrusted to you."* Peter is saying that ministry and the people in the church belong to God and that God entrusts them to us. When you understand that God wants to use you to serve His people, it changes how you view people. It changes how you view your commitment to serve and the things that you do behind the scenes that no one will ever see. You do all these things as unto the Lord, because it is a privilege and a gift.

Spiritual Leaders Are Examples
In verse three, Peter reminds us of another piece of servanthood, *"serving as examples."* In the house of God, we need to have godly men and women that are examples of what the life of Jesus is all about. It's important to know that the moment you start to serve, you become an example, whether you want to or not. Many people are visual learners and when they know you are a follower of God, they are going to look at you and say "if that's what a man of God is, I'm going to follow that. If that's what a dad looks like, I'm going to follow that. If that's what a man who got saved from the drug life does now, I'm going to follow that." They want to see examples of godliness and as you serve, you are an example to them.

Examples are so vital in the church and I know that you may be filled with intense pain because an example that you followed and looked up to fell into some horrible sin. That's a deep wound and it's painful because that person was showing you how to follow Christ. It's a serious thing when a leader falls into sin. Let me encourage you to pray for your pastors and your leaders, that they won't be tempted or snared and do something dumb to tarnish the name of Jesus.

One thing that will help anyone in leadership is adopting something Billy Graham and his team came up with years ago. They called it the Modesto Manifesto, and it has four points.

- **Purity:** Never be alone with someone who is not your spouse, child or parent. This is meant to be practical and not legalistic.

- **Integrity:** Never get involved in the finances of the church. Always be above reproach.

- **Humility:** Never speak negatively of another ministry. This doesn't refer to churches teaching false doctrine, but never raise up your church as the only church or best church.

- **Honesty:** Always be honest in reporting what God is doing.

We take these ideas to heart as leaders because we take leadership seriously. If they worked for Billy Graham for 50 years, they can work for us now. Keep this in mind: a good example doesn't mean a perfect example. There will always be episodic issues in our lives that we will need to work through, but overall, if you want to serve, God needs you with deep integrity and character. This comes from your personal, daily relationship with Him, because the deeper that is, the more progress that you'll make as a servant of the Lord.

Serving is Rewarding

We're at the end of our verse now, and here's what Peter has to encourage us with:

> ...And when the chief shepherd appears you will receive the crown of glory that does not fade away. (1 Peter 5:4)

As hard as serving might be, with all the pitfalls and difficulties and self-denial, there is a reward to look forward to in heaven! Even more, there are often rewards on earth. There's nothing greater than seeing a marriage rescued, or kids walking with the Lord, or seeing people that the whole world wrote off get saved. There's nothing more rewarding than seeing God work in the lives of people, than seeing the Word of God change and transform lives.

THINK ABOUT IT

Serving God is a privilege! I pray that these principles would become ingrained in your heart and your mind. I pray that you'll take time to meditate on these truths and grasp them with great joy today.

CHAPTER 5

TIMOTHY

AN EXAMPLE TO FOLLOW

We spent the last chapter learning about the excellent example in the life of Peter. Now we are going to focus on someone who learned from *his spiritual leader,* Timothy. While Peter learned directly from Jesus—Timothy learned from Paul the apostle. It's clear that what he learned made him a great servant.

We meet Paul in the book of Philippians. He is in prison, chained to a guard, and unable to do what he believes is his ministry—going from church to church to encourage, help, and deal with problems. Paul has heard that the church in Philippi is not doing well and he is anxious. The church is dealing with false teachers and division, and Paul knows they need help. Since he can't go personally, he is looking for someone to send.

"But I trust in the Lord Jesus to send Timothy to you shortly, that I also may be encouraged when I know your state. For I have no one like-minded, who will sincerely care for your state. For all seek their own, not the things which are of Christ Jesus. But you know his proven character, that as a son with his father he served with me in the gospel. Therefore I hope to send him at once, as soon as I see how it goes with me. But I trust in the Lord that I myself shall also come shortly." (Philippians, 2:19-24)

BE PREPARED TO GO: BE AVAILABLE

When Paul looked around at the people who were closest to him, he was probably wondering who would represent the Lord well, who would represent His heart, and who would sincerely care for the church in Philippi. Timothy stood out. There was something about Paul and Timothy that connected them at the heart level. More than that, Timothy had some outstanding qualities that every servant of God should have!

The first quality he had was *availability*. He was ready to go. God is always searching for a man or woman that He can use:

> *For the eyes of the Lord run to and fro throughout the whole earth, to show Himself strong on behalf of those whose heart is loyal to Him.* (2 Chronicles 16:9)

It was one thing for Paul to present the needs of the church in Philippi to Timothy and ask him to go help—but it was a whole other thing for Timothy *to be available* to go.

Isaiah gives us a great example of this quality in a vision: "I heard the voice of the Lord saying: 'Whom shall I send, and who will go for us?'" (Isaiah 6:8). How does Isaiah respond? "Then I said, Here am I! Send me."

God does not ask about our ability or our inability but about our *availability.* In the church, there will always be needs. As Jesus said, the harvest is plentiful...but unfortunately the laborers are few. There are so many things that simply keep us *too busy* and unavailable to the Lord. You may desire to be available, but it is important to understand that being available isn't only about circumstances. It is also about choice.

What are you doing right now that is preparing you to serve God? Of all the plans on your calendar and all the things that demand your attention—are there things that you do daily and weekly that are preparing you to serve your God? If you have trouble finding something, then you're missing out on a key ingredient in your relationship with God.

I have a deeper question for you: *What is it in your life right now that makes you unavailable to serve?* What holds you back when you hear that clarion call to ministry and service? Is it a job or hobby? Perhaps it's an unconfessed sin or a little hidden thing in your life that you are holding onto and haven't dealt with. It could be pride, or self-importance, or as Jesus reminds us in Luke 21:34, it can be *the cares of this life.*

The antidote for keeping our hearts from getting weighed down by the cares of this life is in Hebrews, where we are reminded:

> *Lay aside every weight, and the sin which so easily ensnares us, and let us run with endurance the race that is set before us.* (Hebrews 12:1)

Timothy was free from encumbrance and ready to go.

POSITIONED TO CARE: READY

Timothy was prepared to serve. Timothy was available to the leaders in his life and available to the Lord. This meant that he was positioned in a place that made him ready. Paul says:

> *I have no one like-minded who will sincerely care for you in your state. For all seek their own and not the things which are of Christ Jesus.* (Philippians 2:20)

To me, this is one of the saddest scriptures in the Bible. Paul is basically saying that with the exception of Timothy in this season of his life, *there was no one else who was like-minded* and ready to care for the believers in Philippi.

Timothy was there to serve Paul and support him in his work for the Kingdom. As we read the Bible, we find no mention of Timothy having a desire to usurp Paul or take advantage of his weaknesses. Timothy seemed to have a very good understanding of how to support and serve in the role and position God had given him.

The great Leonard Bernstein was once asked which instrument in the orchestra was the most difficult to play. He thought for a moment and answered "Second fiddle. I can get plenty of first violinists, but to find someone who can play the second fiddle with enthusiasm? That's a problem! And if we have no second fiddle, we have no harmony."

In the church, we need more *second fiddle* believers whose aim in life is to serve completely, unconcerned about positions or titles. These believers are ready to keep the harmony as they serve Jesus. When you seek to serve—be like Timothy—be a blessing to your pastor and those that serve around you.

What Really Matters to Jesus

Jesus invested His life in very specific ways. When we look at Him, we can easily *see* where His heart was. If your desire is to serve Jesus—to serve in your church and in your community and to make a difference—it will be easy to do when you know what mattered most to Jesus.

Luke 4:18-19 gives us a clear picture of what matters to Jesus:

> *The Spirit of the Lord is upon Me, because He has anointed Me to preach the gospel to the poor; He has sent Me to heal the brokenhearted, to preach deliverance to the captives and recovery of sight to the blind, to set at liberty those who are oppressed; and to preach the acceptable year of the Lord.*

Believers Walking in the Spirit Matter to Jesus
In Luke 4:18 Jesus tells us, "The Spirit of the Lord is upon Me." When you serve God, He doesn't want you to serve in your own strength and wisdom, but in the power of the Spirit of God. It matters to God that you are a man or woman filled with the Holy Spirit, baptized by the Holy Spirit, and engulfed in the power of God.

The Poor Matter to Jesus
God cares about the poor practically and spiritually. You can extend that care as His servant. You can serve individually and with our churches with finances, food, opportunities,

and more. You can look around for those who are poor in spirit and seek to fill the spiritual need.

The Brokenhearted Matter to Jesus
If you are wrestling with sorrow and sadness, Jesus cares and desires to extend encouragement and hope to you. This is a job His church should fill as well.

The Captives Matter to Jesus
There are many ways to be captive. You can be captive in jail, paying the consequence for your criminal activities; and you can be captive to addictions, in a prison of your own making. The Bible warns us that if we present ourselves to sin, we become slaves to it. Some of you may be captive in your minds, filled with fear, anxiety and things that trouble you. Jesus cares about those that are in captivity.

The Blind Matter to Jesus
In this passage, we see that Jesus preaches recovery of sight to the blind. This is a physical healing although there is spiritual blindness as well. God is still a healing God, and He desires to heal those who are captive physically and spiritually.

The Oppressed Matter to Jesus
If you are oppressed, Jesus wants to give you liberty and freedom from the pressures that worry you and the things that have entrapped you.

The World Matters to Jesus
In verse 19, Jesus says that *"He came to proclaim the acceptable year of the Lord."* Jesus is saying that the Messiah *has come. That* is the message the church preaches over and over again.

It matters to Jesus that His church genuinely cares for people and loves them, serving them well in His name. The church's love must be untainted by any worldly, selfish ambition. When you pray about serving and when you desire to serve, you must walk in the Spirit and care about the things Jesus cares about. You must grow in maturity. The beautiful thing about maturity is that God gives it to us along with the love for things that He loves and hate for the sinful things that He hates. When you grow to care about the things that God cares about, you begin to grieve and mourn over your own sin, asking God to help you grow so that He can use you. You also begin to long for spiritual nourishment and become willing to say, do, or go wherever He directs you. Most of all, you long for Jesus to return!

PROVEN TO BE FAITHFUL (TRUSTWORTHY)

Timothy had all of those things in abundance, along with another quality. He had a proven character. In Philippians 2:22 it says:

> *But you know his proven character, that as a son with his father he served with me in the Gospel. Therefore I hope to send him at once, as soon as I see how it goes with me. But I trust in the Lord that I myself shall also come shortly.*

The word *proven* means "tested." The idea behind the word proven is that of a metal-smith. The metal-smith would heat up a cauldron of molten silver or gold, and gradually turn the fire up. As the metal heated, the impurities rose to the top and got skimmed off. This process continued until the fire was as hot as it could get, and the metal had no more impurities rising to the surface. The metal-smith knew that he was done when the metal became mirror-like and he could see his own reflection in the surface.

It's easy to talk like a Christian, to mention Bible verses, and talk about the fruit of the Spirit—but when you actually *want* those things to be lived out in your daily life, God will help you. He will allow situations to come into your life that require the fruit of the Spirit.

It's great when we pass those tests and walk in the spirit. Often we will also fail, and that can be difficult. Keep in mind that when you fail, God is revealing a place in your character that needs His attention.

Your character is who you are when you're alone and think no one is watching. Sometimes character is confused with reputation. *Reputation* is what people think about you, but *character* is who you are; it grows when you are tested.

When you serve Jesus, you want your character and reputation to be the same. You do not want to be two different people. The Bible calls that hypocrisy. Dwight L. Moody said it well, "If I take care of my character, God will take care of my reputation."

As a young man, Timothy's reputation and character were the same. His character was *proven*. Timothy must have gone through a lot to get to that place. There are no shortcuts to a proven character. When tough circumstances come to your life, remember that God is not punishing you or teasing you. He will use those circumstances to develop your character.

William Barclay said, "Timothy's great value was that he was always willing to go anywhere. In his hands was a message as safe as if Paul had delivered it himself. Others might be consumed with selfish ambition, but not Timothy. Timothy's one desire was to serve Paul and Jesus Christ. He becomes the example [patron saint] of all those who are content with second place, as long as they can serve" (From William Barclay's Daily Study Bible).

Timothy was prepared to go, positioned to care, and proven to be faithful. He was a very good example for us.

Who We Are is Far More Important Than What We Do

There is an inseparable link between the character of a church and the spiritual depth and quality of its leadership and servants. They define its progress, and it shows us an important spiritual truth: *Who we are in our relationship with Jesus Christ is far more important that what we do for Jesus.*

In Luke chapter 6:39-40, Jesus shows us this idea with a parable:

> *And He spoke a parable to them. "Can the blind lead the blind? Will they not both fall into the ditch? A disciple is not above his teacher, but everyone who is perfectly trained will be like his teacher."*

Jesus probably had the Pharisees in mind when He taught this. It was meant as a rebuke to them because they were religious rulers who were out of touch with God and leading others down their dark path, like blind guides. The result was suffering.

It's spiritually important to be careful in whom you listen to—because you are going to become like them. You want to be following men and women who represent and reflect the very character and nature of God, because serving Jesus is a very serious thing. Any true teacher of God's Word will yield to the Holy Spirit, and they will be filled with the Spirit of God. Why? Because the ultimate teacher, according to the Bible, is the Spirit of God...given to all believers when Jesus left earth:

> *But the Helper, The Holy Spirit, whom the Father will send in My name, he will teach you all things, and bring to your remembrance all things that I said to you.* (John 14:26)

THINK ABOUT IT

As you prepare yourselves to step out to serve, consider Timothy. He was a young man at that time, yet God used him greatly. God wants to use you, no matter what age you are. He would have you become that man or woman of proven character, prepared to serve, positioned in the right place to care and ready to go out.

It's my prayer that as you recognize the calling of God in your lives and the need for spiritual service, that you will be a person who serves God wholeheartedly, holding nothing back. I pray that you will be ready, prepared, and available, sincerely caring for God and those around you. I pray that God will pour out His Spirit upon us in these last days and that you will be after His own heart in love and forgiveness.

CHAPTER 6

TWELVE BIBLICAL TRUTHS:

THE MINISTRY OF SERVANTHOOD

Studying and learning about serving Jesus never gets tiring, does it? We've spent five chapters looking at insights from the Bible that will make us greater vessels in the hand of God. None of these things are *new* or *novel*. We are simply allowing the Bible to speak to us. The things we have learned have challenged, stirred, and stretched us—they have encouraged and uplifted us and prepared us to step into serving Jesus Christ, both in our churches and in the world. *These principles of servanthood transcend every pastor and movement of churches.*

This study is all about *getting at the very heart of God in serving His people.* One way we can understand God's heart is through the process of discipleship.

2 Timothy 2:2 says it this way:

> *And the things which you have heard from me among many witnesses, commit these to faithful men who will be able to teach others also.*

This is a great description of the *process of discipleship,* something that I've experienced personally. My pastor handed down the things he had learned from his pastor on to me; his pastor handed down what he had learned from his pastor, and so on.

TWO WAYS TO LEARN

There are two ways you can learn things. You can learn things the easy way, or you can learn them the hard way. A lot of my ministry experience has been by learning things the hard way. At times I have been so eager to do things for the Lord and to step out in faith in obedience to God that, with my personality, sometimes came mistakes. I've definitely made my fair share. I've also had my fair share of conversations with pastors and leaders who cared enough to look me in the eye and let me know where I needed to change.

In this chapter, I'm going to share twelve things that I've personally learned through those difficult times of ministry, things that continue to be a great help to me yet today. It's my prayer that they will take root in your heart and help point you in the right direction as you serve the Lord in your churches and in the world. All of these ideas are rooted in the Word of God. The first four are *spiritually foundational*—the rest of the principles will build on these four *practically.*

1

WE SERVE GOD IN THE SPIRIT
NOT IN OUR OWN STRENGTH

As you've been going through this book of practical instruction, you might have been inspired to go out and buy a book on leadership so that you could learn more about leadership and serving. Now that you know a little, the temptation might be to *jump in and start serving with both feet.*

Here's where our first principle comes in: Every person serving God must be rooted in the Spirit of God, indwelt by the Spirit of God, empowered by the Spirit of God, and not with worldly wisdom.

There's a problem all of us share to one degree or another: *we all tend to think we know more than we really do, especially spiritually.* The Bible says it this way:

> *If anyone thinks that he knows anything, he knows nothing yet, as he ought to know.* (1 Corinthians 8:2)

The Bible is clear: There is always a place of growth for us. There is always a place of new wisdom and new understanding, and it comes from the Spirit of God. Ultimately, we need to be careful not to serve God in our own flesh. Methodologies and practical principles can be helpful, but our ultimate goal is to be open to the Lord and all that He wants, flowing in His Spirit and walking according to His will. Zechariah 4:6 is such an important Scripture for every servant of Jesus:

> *"Not by might, not by power, but by My Spirit," says the Lord of hosts.*

2

WE SERVE GOD WITH HIS WISDOM
NOT OUR OWN UNDERSTANDING

The key to walking in the Spirit is living in God's wisdom.
There would be far less confusion and hurt feelings, far
fewer mistakes and injured people, if we would lean on the
Lord and not our own understanding. This is especially
important when you and I are giving spiritual counsel.

Here at Calvary Aurora we call this *spiritual discipleship.* If
you have a need and sit down with a pastor, that pastor is
going to open up God's Word to you, because we believe
that through that encounter you are going to grow in the
things of God. For the sake of understanding, we can also
call this *spiritual counseling.*

If God brings someone to you for counseling, you may
think that you know what he or she is going through because
you've been through that experience as well. Perhaps you
can connect with them emotionally. You may have been
through something traumatic that gives you a sense of
understanding for the situation.

Know this: *You cannot completely understand their issue
or situation.* When you begin to think that you do, you
are stepping aside from God's wisdom and into your own
understanding.

Also, keep this in mind: *You have no idea what that person
is going through...because you are not them. You haven't
lived their life and you don't have their upbringing.* If you
give them help based on understanding their situation, you
will just be giving them *your opinion.* When people come

to believers for an answer, they don't need an opinion; they need God's Word.

Begin by Listening

When you begin to counsel someone, you need to begin by listening. Take home what you hear and pray about it. Open the Word of God. That is how you: "Trust in the Lord with all your heart, and lean not on your own understanding. In all your ways acknowledge Him and He shall direct your paths..." (Proverbs 3:5-6). This is foundational to serving God with His wisdom and not our own understanding.

3

BE A MAN OR A WOMAN
OF THE BIBLE

The degree of effectiveness you will have in serving God and people will be directly related to how much of the Bible is in your life. You need to *know the heart of God* as you serve, and that's why you need to be a man or woman of the Bible. If you have very little time, or if you have very little interest in the Word of God, you're going to make a poor servant of God. You can't serve Him without the tools He has provided for the job, and one main tool that God has given us is His Word.

Something I encourage those that I serve with:

> *Read your Bible every day. We can read a lot of great books about the bible, but unless you know the Book, the books about the Book are worthless. Read it. Take it. Have it. Use it. I can guarantee that it will increase your effectiveness as a servant of the Lord.*

Paul encourages the young Timothy in the ministry and service that God has called him to in this passage:

> *But you must continue in the things which you have learned and been assured of, knowing from whom you have learned them; that from childhood you have known the Holy Scriptures, which are able to make you wise for salvation through faith which is in Jesus Christ. All Scripture is given by inspiration of God and is profitable for doctrine, for reproof, for instruction, for correction in righteousness, that the man of God may be complete, thoroughly equipped for every good work.* (2 Timothy 3:14-17)

Timothy was a man of the Word. This began when he was a child, learning it constantly from his mom and grandma. Their diligence and his continued studies prepared him to go off with Paul onto the mission field and pastor a church. The Scripture is a profitable and important tool for men and women of God.

Do you need a question answered? Turn to the Bible. Are you giving counsel or advice? Use the Bible. One of the best things you can do to make yourself a better, more fruitful servant of Jesus is to be a man or woman of *one Book!*

4

BE A MAN AND WOMAN OF PRAYER

Prayer and the Bible go hand-in-hand, and if you get this right, it will greatly help you in serving Jesus. The Scriptures tell us to "Pray without ceasing..." (1 Thessalonians 5:17).

We can always improve on our prayer life. Commit to pray about everything.

Pray for people; Pray *about* people
Pray for yourself
Pray for your church
Pray for your pastors and leaders
Pray for your president, senator, governor, and mayor.

If you have an issue or a question, pray about it and open the Word of God. He will give you direction.

The key to walking in the Spirit, and accomplishing the work of God is to be in constant communication with God, both receiving from the Word of God and giving in prayer.

5

Strive to Maintain the Unity of the Spirit
and the Bond of Peace

This point may seem a little complex, but it's just the Bible's way of saying, "Don't be divisive." If you want to be a good leader or a good servant, then don't be a tool of the enemy and bring division into God's church.

Sometimes you will disagree with other people, or have a problem with someone else in the church (maybe even a pastor or overseer). If you are in that position, don't be divisive. Go to them directly, as soon as possible, and work it out. Handle the situation biblically. We talked about this a little in chapter 3 of this book. Matthew chapter 18 gives us the pattern to follow: *Go to the person and work it out. This is important: if you can't work it out, be careful. While giving God time to work things out, don't try to build a case.*

Don't begin going to and fro to different people with gossip and slander and bringing someone's name through the mud, just to get others on your side. Just don't do it.

As a servant, as a leader, *be a peacemaker.* Jesus gave a promise. He said "Blessed are the peacemakers..." (Matthew 5:9). And if you can't agree with the leadership where you are, let me encourage you to find a more like-minded ministry where you can serve your heart out in unity.

Paul told the Romans this: "If it is possible, as much as depends on you, live peaceably with all men..." (Romans 12:18). Nothing does more damage, harm, and destruction than division, especially in the church. God has some strong words for people who are divisive:

> *"These six things the Lord hates, yes seven are an abomination to Him: a proud look, a lying tongue, hands that shed innocent blood, a heart that devises wicked plans, feet that are swift to running to evil, a false witness that speaks lies, **and one who sews discord among brethren.**"* (Proverbs 6:16-19)

God hates the sewing of discord. To put it in a more modern way: "God hates those that divide and cause division."

Don't do it, especially as you step up to serve in your church. Take time to work things out. Grow together with your church body. Of course there are differences, and mistakes will be made. When those things happen, that's where grace comes in. *If you give your leadership time, and if they give you time, they will work it out as unto the Lord.* Then His glory and His kingdom, and the Name and reputation that He has will be glorified on the Earth, because of the love that's manifested in His church. *Strive to maintain the unity of the Spirit and the bond of peace.*

6

LAY ASIDE AND CRUCIFY PREJUDICE
IT'S NOT JESUS!

Jesus Christ was not a prejudiced man, but His creation was and is very prejudiced. The idea behind prejudice is that you *pre-judge* someone, elevating yourself above them, because of something that you *see*. Perhaps it's the color of their skin, financial status, where they grew up, where they live, what they look like, what they smell like, or what they're into. No matter what it is, prejudice doesn't make sense. It's unlovely, ungracious, unkind, hurtful, and harmful...and it's very disruptive. *If you are going to serve Jesus, then you cannot be a prejudiced person.*

In 1 Samuel 16:6-7 it says:

> *...But the Lord said to Samuel, "Do not look at his appearance or at the height of his stature, because I have refused him; for the Lord does not see as man sees, for man looks at the outward appearance, but the Lord looks at the heart."*

This verse is so important because it makes it clear that, as humans, we look at the outward appearance of a person. That's all we have to look at, because we can't see the heart. *This is a warning to be careful—because what you see may not lead you to the right conclusions.* You have no idea what's going on behind the scenes in the heart.

In Heaven, we will see people from every tribe, tongue, and nation. You know what that tells me? It tells me that the love of God is very broad. The love of God goes to people that are wrestling and struggling with sin right now.

His love is ready to break through and make absolutely any human into a new creation with a relationship with Christ.

Keep this in mind: prejudice harms the Gospel of Jesus Christ. The Gospel can change people's lives. The Gospel can change cities. The Gospel can change nations. The Gospel of Jesus Christ has literally changed the world...and that's what every servant of Jesus wants to be a part of. Lay aside and crucify any prejudice that you have, and if you have gotten off track here, pray and He will get you back on track.

7

SERVE WILLINGLY
WITHOUT MURMURING AND COMPLAINING

Murmuring and complaining have been with us since biblical days. Let me clarify: complaining is a waste of time. It doesn't solve any problems. It doesn't build anyone up. It doesn't help anyone. It doesn't free anyone from any bondage. It doesn't deal with any hard issues. What it can do is take a real faithful, healthy servant of God and propel them into the flesh, making him *unusable*.

This applies when you are at work, too. When you complain at work, what does it accomplish? Usually nothing. In fact, it just makes things worse. It makes you feel miserable. Have you noticed that complainers are usually surrounded by other complainers? Complaining burns you out, because you're only focused on the negative side of things. I think complaining is one of those temptations that gets thrown our way in different seasons of life, and we've all been guilty.

How to Get Back on Track

When you want to complain, you need to get back on track. You can do this practically by looking to the needs of others. Look for someone who needs prayer and pray with them. If you see somebody crying, go ask them how they're doing. If you see trash that needs to be picked up, pick it up. If you see something you can't fix, then bring it to the attention of someone that can fix it. This will save you from that complaining spirit.

Let me be clear: When you're complaining in one area, you will complain about everything, and it will sap the joy out of a willing servant and faithful person.

I love the simplicity of the Bible, and what it says about complaining is easy to understand:

> *Do all things without complaining and disputing, that you may become blameless and harmless children of God without fault in the midst of a crooked and a perverse generation, among whom you shine as lights in the world.* (Philippians 2:14-16)

The Bible is clear: a lack of complaining and murmuring actually makes you more useful in a very dark world. It's one thing to complain about something—it's a whole other thing to stand up and make a difference for Jesus and shine as a light in a very dark world.

8

TOSS YOUR AGENDA OUT THE DOOR
GET ON BOARD WITH THE AGENDA GOD HAS GIVEN YOUR CHURCH OR MINISTRY

If God has called you into a certain church, be careful that *as you serve, you don't lose track and begin serving a personal agenda.* The only difference between Bible-believing, Bible-teaching, God-honoring churches isn't so much the doctrine. It's the philosophy of ministry that makes them different. Each one has a flavor, or an atmosphere.

On the Leadership Side
Most leaders are totally open for a fresh work of God. What we're *not* open to is someone coming in and wanting to push their agenda. He has raised our church up from *nothing.* When you become part of a church, you must submit that to the Lord, and trust that He has brought you to a church where you will bear fruit. I want to let you know that it's okay if you have a *different vision of ministry.* Just understand, that it *may not be for that body of believers.* It doesn't mean it's bad; it doesn't mean it's not from the Lord; it just means *that it may not fit.*

A Focused Church
Churches need to be very focused on what God wants them to do. That means there are a lot of things they should not do in order to stay focused.

Discipleship, evangelism, and sending people out are the focus of *our* church. Anything that distracts us from those things will not fit.

> *Can two walk together unless they are agreed?*
> (Amos 3:3)

You may come to the leadership with a vision that God has given to you and they will encourage you and pray for you and see what God wants to do. But be careful that you don't go in this church or any other church and *try to push an agenda*. Instead, pray for God to send you to the right place—or, seek to work together with the ministry that God is already doing, as a co-laborer, with like-mindedness as we discussed in chapter 3.

9

REMEMBER...GOD RAISES UP ONE
AND PUTS DOWN ANOTHER

Remember that positions, titles, and responsibilities come from the Lord and not from man. When you serve in a church, canvas for position, attempt to work some political angle to get a place or a position, gather a following, or attempt to tear someone else's ministry down so that *you* can climb the ministry ladder...*will not go well   because there's no ladder to climb.*

If you're a servant in your church, *then serve* and leave all the other stuff to the Lord. No leadership team is actively looking for people to fill titles and responsibilities.

As a pastoral team and a leadership team, we are actively looking for God's anointing and gifting in your life. How are you wired? What's your heart? How do you serve? Are you a man of the Word, or a woman of the Bible? Do you pray? Are you a spiritual man, or nonspiritual? Those are the things we are looking for. Once we see them, then our responsibility is to make sure you're in a place where you can bear fruit for the Kingdom.

Psalm 75:7 was given to me at a time in my life where I felt passed over in ministry. It says: "But God is the judge; He puts down one and exalts another..." I know it's hard sometimes to get the "No." But sometimes you will face a "no," and *you'll have to accept that it came through God first.*

I don't know what God's doing in your life, but I can tell you this: *God is doing something, and if He's raised you up, then that's from the Him. If He's put you down, then that's from Him.* You can trust that God is bigger than your pastor, your spiritual leader, your boss, or your supervisor. God is bigger, and because God is bigger, you can trust Him with every area of your life. Focus on serving Him and let Him use you.

10

HANDLE CHURCH CONFLICTS BIBLICALLY

If you're going to serve in a church, you need to learn how to solve things biblically. When a disagreement comes up, you may try to gain someone's approval. You may try to get a group around you, and in the process you are trying to put someone else down. The problem doing it that way is that those methods are *not from the Lord.* Matthew chapter 18 gives us the pathway to biblical conflict resolution:

> *"If your brother has sinned against you,"* Jesus said, *"go to him, you and him alone and share the matter with him; if he hears you, you have won your brother."* (Matthew 18:15)

At times, when conflict comes, people run away from it. Running away is not in the Scriptures either. Instead, God calls us to work on the problem—pray through it, asking

God for reconciliation and restoration. Humble yourself before the mighty hand of God, and let *Him* lift you up.

Another Scripture where we see conflict resolution is in 2 Timothy 2:24:

> *A servant of the Lord must not quarrel, but be gentle to all, able to teach, patient in humility, correcting those who are in opposition, if perhaps God will grant them repentance so that they may know the truth.*

As a servant of Jesus, with the heart of Jesus, handle your conflicts in the church biblically, and be a peacemaker.

Finally, I will add that the result of biblical conflict resolution isn't always what you expect. The other party may not always agree with you. Instead of reconciliation and forgiveness, they may run away. No matter what they do, you and I as servants of Jesus need our consciences to be clear before God. Most of the time though, when you take time to talk, pray, cry, and work through it, God gets the glory because there will be reconciliation and forgiveness.

11

WITHHOLD NOTHING FROM THE LORD

A common trap of those that serve in the church is the idea that "since I serve, I don't have to give in other areas." One example of this is in the realm of giving of tithes and offerings. Some servants say: "I don't give my tithes and offerings financially anymore to this church, because my time is my tithe, and so I give my time."

As a pastor I have to ask, "Where in the Bible did you find that?" The answer of course is *nowhere*. The reality is that your time, your talents, your resources, your money, and everything else belong to the Lord.

Here's what happens when you have that mindset: you are literally withholding from God what belongs to Him: your time, your talents, and your gifts. You are still in control of them. Be careful there. *Your time is not your tithe.* Your time doesn't even belong to you, and neither does your tithe. They belong to the Lord.

Give yourself wholly and totally to the Lord and serve faithfully.

> *"But this I say, he who sows sparingly will also reap sparingly; and he who sows bountifully will also reap bountifully."* (2 Corinthians 9:6)

If you are serving in a church, and stop giving faithfully to the Lord in other areas, it doesn't make sense. That choice is inconsistent with the heart of a true servant.

Remember This
Your serving the Lord actually began with your giving. Giving to God is what motivated you to give of your gifts and talents in the first place. *Continue to withhold nothing from the Lord. Give yourself completely to Him, and serve Him with joy and gladness in everything.*

12

ATTEND SERVICES
RECEIVE GOD'S WORD FROM YOUR PASTOR

This is our final and very important point: *Be in the church services, receiving the Word of God from your pastor regularly and consistently.* This point is in the context of serving, because when you step up and begin to serve you can get so busy serving (there may seem to be so many needs) that before you know it, you stop sitting in the services with your family, your wife and your kids, and taking notes.

Do you remember in the beginning, when you first got saved? You were eating up the Bible! You were reading it, studying it, circling and highlighting Scriptures! You were learning, growing, sharing, and talking about it all the time. It was awesome!

Then you started serving, and all of that went downhill because *now you're so busy serving.* You may even have a position of spiritual leadership that keeps you out of the sanctuary. Watch out, because the next thing you know, you won't be talking about the things of the Lord anymore *because you're not regularly receiving the Word from your pastor.*

Even worse, you're not in the environment of the saints. Peter told us: "Shepherd the flock of God that is among you" (1 Peter 5:2). Serving doesn't mean we pull away from the very people that God has called us to serve.

You never want to stop, because you don't want to go backwards. If you are ever serving so much that you can't sit in the services...maybe you need to step away from that ministry. *Being in the service is more important than stepping away from the very place that feeds you so you can grow.* That will take you backwards, and it's a trap.

Every church is looking for people that have a heart for the Lord, a heart for the church, and a heart for ministry. They are looking for people who are serving their hearts out, as unto the Lord. In Mark 12:37 It says, "And the common people heard Him gladly." That verse means that the ministry of Jesus was accepted by everyone, but I love that last phrase "gladly." It depicts to us that it should be a joy to receive the Word of God.

If the enemy can ever disconnect you from your pastor, you're in a very dangerous place. Not that the pastor has authority or lords over you, but if you aren't able to grow through the teaching of God's Word, you have to go find a place where you *are* going to grow. Your spiritual growth is linked to your service to God, and it is important to the heart of God and to His kingdom.

THINK ABOUT IT

The material in these six chapters reflect the things I wish someone had told me as a new believer, so I wouldn't have had to learn them in the school of hard knocks.

These truths are simple, yet we tend to forget them in the busyness of life and ministry. I hope this study will enable you to serve with gladness, and to make these truths part of your life.

I pray that you grew through this study, that the fruit of your life in serving is sweet, that God continues to use your church in the metro area and around the state and around the world. I pray that as you continue to take radical, crazy steps that are beyond you, beyond your abilities; that you trust Him and hold fast to Him and that you are that blessed person that we see here:

> *"Who walks not in the counsel of the ungodly, nor stands in the path of sinners, nor sits in the seat of the scornful! But his delight is in the law of the Lord, and in his law he meditates day and night, and he (or she) shall be like a tree planted by the rivers of water, that brings forth its fruit in its season, whose leaf also shall not wither; and whatever he does, shall prosper."* (Psalm 1:1-3)

Connect with Ed Taylor

Mailing Address:

Calvary Aurora
18900 E. Hampden Ave.
Aurora, CO 80013

Phone:

303-628-7200

Websites:

edtaylor.org
calvaryaurora.org

Email:

pastored@calvaryaurora.org

Social Media:

Facebook: pastoredt@facebook.com
Twitter: @CalvaryAurora
Instagram: @ed4thelord

Abounding Grace Media

18900 E. HAMPDEN AVE • AURORA, CO 80013 • (303) 628-7200

82830799R00048

Made in the USA
Columbia, SC
06 December 2017